EASY Guide to <u>Upgrade</u> your Communication,
Presentation and Public Speaking Skills

I0476393

The 7 Steps
to
START
Speaking
Professionally

Based on

Proudly shared with you by

DEDICATION

To my father, Dr. Manikrao Waghchoude,
for his
deep love, care, and trust in me

Success Coach Nilesh at Press event, 2014

CONGRATULATIONS

Ability to speak professionally is one of the most Powerful Skills. **Many want it but very few get it.** Being expert in this arena will reap **massive rewards.** Therefore it is worth putting your time, money and resources in building you, as the World class speaker.

Congratulations on starting this journey. I know it will change your life and lives of the people those will be touched by your message.

All the Best!

Yours Sincerely,
Success Coach Nilesh

www.SuccessCoachNilesh.com

CONTENTS

ACKNOWLEDGMENTS

As Rumi, a 13th century Persian poet, has said, "You are not living on earth, you are passing through earth."

For my journey on earth, I am blessed to meet certain people who have helped me shape my life.

I would first like to thank my wife Meenal for patiently listening to my dreams and ambitions and for supporting my numerous attempts to make this book a best experience for you, the reader. She is one of my first audience.

I would also like to thank my sister, Neelima, my brother-in-law and friend Jeevan, my mother Sunita, and my brother Sanket for their love and care.

Next, a huge thanks to my friends, clients and all the people who have helped me bring this book to you.

Everyone matters.

ABOUT THE AUTHOR . . .

Nilesh Waghchoude (also known as Success Coach Nilesh) is the best-selling Author, International Speaker and creator of Accelerated Success Techniques®.

He has spoken at London Youth Conference, London Business School, Bradford School of Management, College of Engineering Pune- COEP, YASHADA Pune, Lila Poonawala Foundation, Maharashtra Mandal London, Junior Chamber International, UK etc.

He has also travelled and spoken in many countries around the world.

He has coached and consulted CEOs, Directors, Managers, Students, Entrepreneurs etc.

However he started from very bottom. Nilesh was born and brought up in India where English was not even his first language. After Studying at village and Taluka levels he moved to Pune (One of the big cities in India) to study engineering. He was overwhelmed by the people and life in the city because he had never experienced that before. He had lack of self-confidence, self-doubt and negative beliefs. He even failed in his first year engineering exam. However he kept going and graduated in engineering with a first class plus distinction.

Nilesh started his professional career as a Car Design Engineer. After working in India for a couple of years he went to the USA to work for his company's clients.

His professional career was great but he wanted to pursue his dream of completing MBA. To achieve his dream he quit his job and went to the United Kingdom for his Business studies.

After completing his MBA, he got a job offer to work for one of the most prestigious luxury car companies in the UK and he started his job. He was very happy with his job, but this happiness didn't last long. Something was going to happen which transformed his life forever.

Due to the economic recession, his company undertook the lay-offs route. As Nilesh was fairly new in his job; he was amongst the people who got laid off.

This was a massive setback for Nilesh. He had a huge education loan to pay back and there were no signs of the economy recovering. He applied for thousands of jobs and what he got was only rejections.

Nothing seemed to be working for him. Nilesh began to think: How did he get here? How can he come out of this mess, survive and be successful?

At that moment he made a decision to change his bad situation and work diligently to become successful in his career.

He then started working part time for a very low paying job at Arts Centre where his job was to check the tickets at the door of the venue.

During this time Nilesh also started his own Business consulting company. He realized that 'It's not our circumstances but our decisions that shape our lives & our future'.

In his free time he started reading self-development books and listening to audio programs. He even attended LIVE training sessions, seminars and workshops by world-class people such as Tony Robbins, Les Brown, Harv Eker, Richard Branson, Donald Trump, Robert Kiyosaki, Brain Tracy etc. and his life started to get back on track.

Nilesh's perseverance resulted in him starting to deliver successful coaching and training sessions that transformed the life of many individuals and businesses.

During the first year of the company he was the finalist for two prestigious awards by the Institute of Business Consulting UK.

(Best Newcomer to Consulting and Most Outstanding Achievement towards Continuous Professional Development)

Nilesh now takes Trainings, Consulting and one to one coaching sessions.

Nilesh teaches those Precise, Proven and Powerful Tools & Strategies which will help you make FASTER Progress in your Career, Business and Life.

Using the principles he now teaches, Nilesh has transformed his own life, career, finances, health, and relationships.

He now works with professionals from all over the world to provide them smart strategies to make faster progress in their lives & businesses.

These strategies are made up of several critical secrets absolutely necessary for **rapid & sustainable** personal, professional and business success.

So please don't even think of missing the information revealed in his books and sessions.

For further details on his sessions, trainings & workshops please visit:

www.SuccessCoachNilesh.com

So far Nilesh has helped his clients in following areas:

- ✓ Increasing their Income by 40-300% by his Efficient Money Management System (EMMS)
- ✓ Improving their Leadership, Communication, Public Speaking and Time Management skills to achieve Maximum Influence and Results in shorter time
- ✓ Developing Powerful Action Plans to Become More Efficient and Productive
- ✓ Building their own Businesses from Concept to Reality (C2R) in less than 30 days
- ✓ Feeling Confident at Work place and Achieving Maximum Results
- ✓ Getting freedom from Fears and Stress
- ✓ Increasing their Savings by 20-50% by his Strategic Financial Planning (SFP)
- ✓ Achieving their Personal Goals and Becoming Successful Strategically & Quickly
- ✓ Developing Marketing & Sales Strategies which will work in real life to achieve Business Turnaround & Long Lasting Growth
- ✓ Becoming an Expert to make Faster Progress in their Career and Life
- ✓ Gaining Confidence & Power during Interviews.
- ✓ Designing Personal Blueprint for Long-term Success
- ✓ & Many More topics to suit his clients' Special Needs

For further details on his sessions, trainings & workshops please visit:

www.SuccessCoachNilesh.com

*** This Book has been made available for FREE download at www.SuccessCoachNilesh.com. Take Your Copy Now!

Meet Nilesh @ . . .

Google:

Success Coach Nilesh

Linked In:

Success Coach Nilesh or Nilesh Waghchoude

Facebook:

- Nilesh Waghchoude

- Success Coach Nilesh (Like us and be part of growing team)

You Tube:

Search by name: Success Coach Nilesh

Slide Share:

Search by name: Success Coach Nilesh

Email:

MySuccess@SuccessCoachNilesh.com

I was ...

I was afraid of Public speaking. I had a huge stage fear.

What if I forget my content? What if someone asks me a difficult question and I can't answer it? What if they don't like my content? How should I dress during my presentation? How should I impress the audience? How should I make my session more inspirational for the audience? How can I start the speech? What should I include in the speech? How should I select my topic? How can I make the session interactive rather than boring for the audience?

I was there. I have been through all this.

If you have asked similar questions to yourself then let me give you an useful update.

You are on the right track. Everybody starts like this.

All the powerful speakers in the world starts like this.

So, you are not alone.

Keep reading and we will transform the way you Speak.

You are about to learn **Accelerated Success Techniques**® in Professional Speaking.

Let's make you the Powerful Professional Speaker.

I am ...

My audience says I'm one of the best speakers they have met.

My audience says they never get bored even for a minute in my sessions. My audience says they have fun, learn a lot, grow as a human being and have lots of breakthroughs. My audience says they would love to bring their friends and families to listen to my sessions. My audience says they get the confidence they are looking for from my sessions.

Your audience will say that too.

I'm not saying this to impress you but to assure you that,

You can be world class.

You can speak internationally.

You can share your message to a large audience

You can transform people's lives and businesses for the better.

You can be an effective leader.

You can be an inspirational messenger.

As I said earlier,

You are about to learn **Accelerated Success Techniques**® in Professional Speaking. Keep reading and we will transform the way you Speak.

What STOPs many people?

The answer is FEAR

People have many types of fear.

The average person ranks 'the fear of public speaking' higher than the fear of death. The truth is, this fear could be hurting your professional and personal life.

You may have been there before. E.g. You feel nervous, your palms sweat, and your stomach ties itself into knots. You don't want to do it. You would rather do anything else than talk to the audience.

Is this you?

In business, it is essential for you to be able to get your point across. It is likely that all of us will one day have to speak in public. Whether we are giving a formal presentation to an audience, or simply asking your boss for a promotion, speaking skills are essential to getting ahead in a professional setting.

The fear of public speaking is very real.

Listed here are things, majority of people are afraid of:

0) Fear of public speaking

1) Fear of darkness

2) Fear of heights

3) Fear of death

4) Fear of failure

5) Fear of rejections

6) Fear of boss

7) Fear of spouse

8) Fear of spiders

9) Fear of commitments

10) Fear of water

11) Fear of falling

12) Fear of being alone

13) Fear of snakes etc.

But amongst all, fear of public speaking get most votes because many people all over the world feel it.

Are you one of them? I guess not. However never mind. We are going to learn how to tame this fear.

Tell me, have you ever experienced any of this while you are on the stage to speak?

Sweating

Stuttering

Rapid breathing

Freezing in front of audience

Forgetting what you have to say

Weak voice

Dry mouth

Rapid heartbeats

Shaking body

Change in blood pressure

If yes, then let me reveal that these are **common symptoms.**

All new speakers go through these.

Now,

Let's move on.

Speaking professionally can help you to:

1) Be seen as an Expert in your field

2) Network effectively

3) Sell your goods and services

4) Ask for promotion

5) Influence your team to get better results

6) Inspire others

7) Confidently present to superiors

8) Share your thoughts on social cause

9) Influence your kids

10) Become well known among your co-workers

So now you know, why speaking professionally is a powerful skill and it is worth putting time, money and energy to master this skill.

It is truly life changing for you and your audience.

How can YOU become World Class?

To help you start your professional speaking journey I am going to introduce you to a powerful model.

Named as **World class Speaker System**™.

It is one of my famous and effective **Accelerated Success Techniques**®.

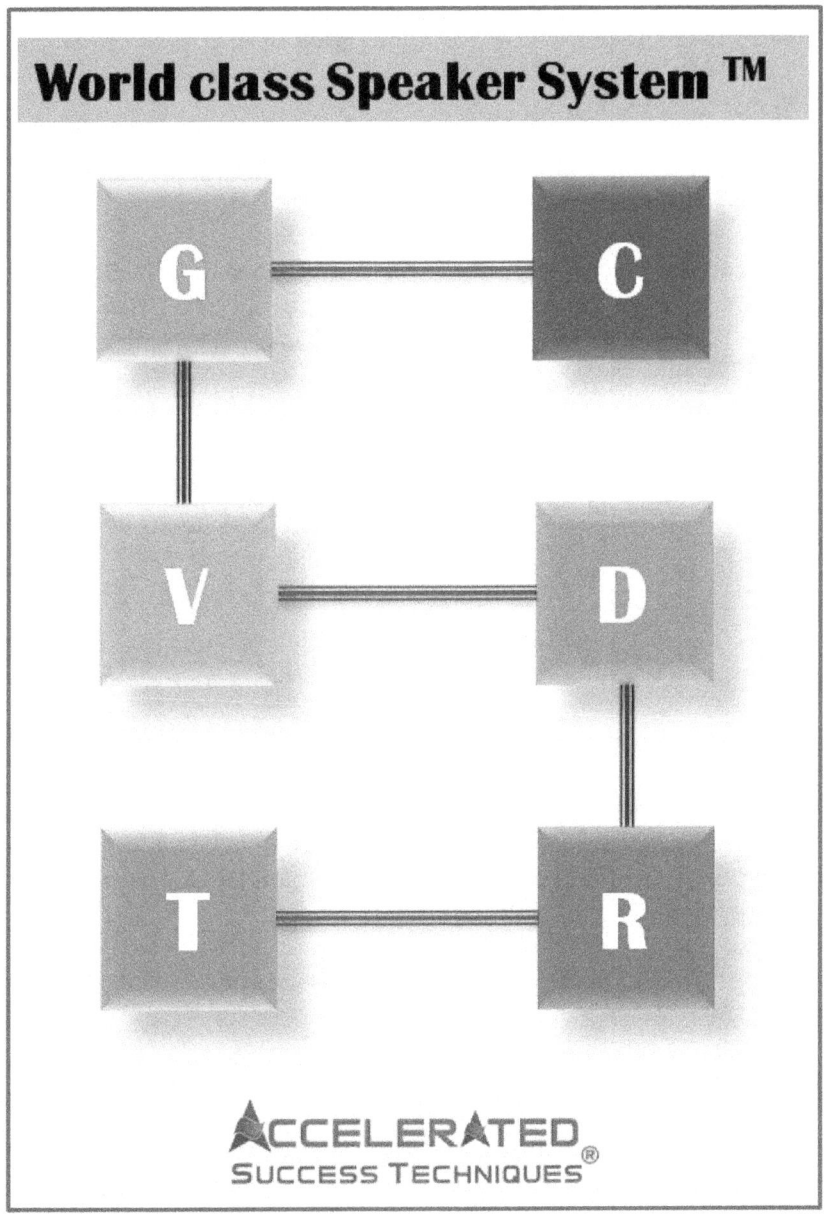

T = Topic, R = Reason, D = Design
V= Visualize, G=Genuine and C = Connect & Deliver
© Success Coach Nilesh

Now,
to get you started let's first understand,

What is Accelerated Success Techniques®?

Accelerated Success Techniques® are the Tools and Strategies put together in a <u>precise sequence</u> which will help you reach faster from where you are to where you want to be.

It can be anywhere in your career, business or life.

Think about your ATM card.
To withdraw money from ATM with your card you need a PIN.

Generally it's a 4 digit PIN.

Now, if you carefully observe this PIN is nothing but any combination of numbers from 0 to 9.

You choose your combination and use that as your PIN.

Now imagine that you went to your favorite shop, did your shopping and now as you are about to pay for your shopping you took your ATM card, put it in the card reader terminal and now you are entering your PIN.

You will need to enter your PIN in <u>precise sequence</u> and you have to use the exact same numbers as your PIN.

The **Accelerated Success Techniques®** are just like that.

You may have heard of some of the random techniques but what you are learning here is the **precise sequence** of these techniques.

In the **World class Speaker System**™ .
I'll share the exact steps in the precise order. As you follow this <u>step by step system</u>; you'll become the Professional speaker.

Yoo-hoo…

Well, my dear friend, Are you ready? Buckle up and let's get started.

Principles shared here may seem to be most aligned to public speaking however these are the similar fundamentals you need to develop for your communication and Presentations skills. Therefore please study all these carefully.

Let's uncover the first 6 Steps . . .

The 1st Step = Master Your Topic

If you are Master of Content; Confidence will easily come.

~   Success Coach Nilesh

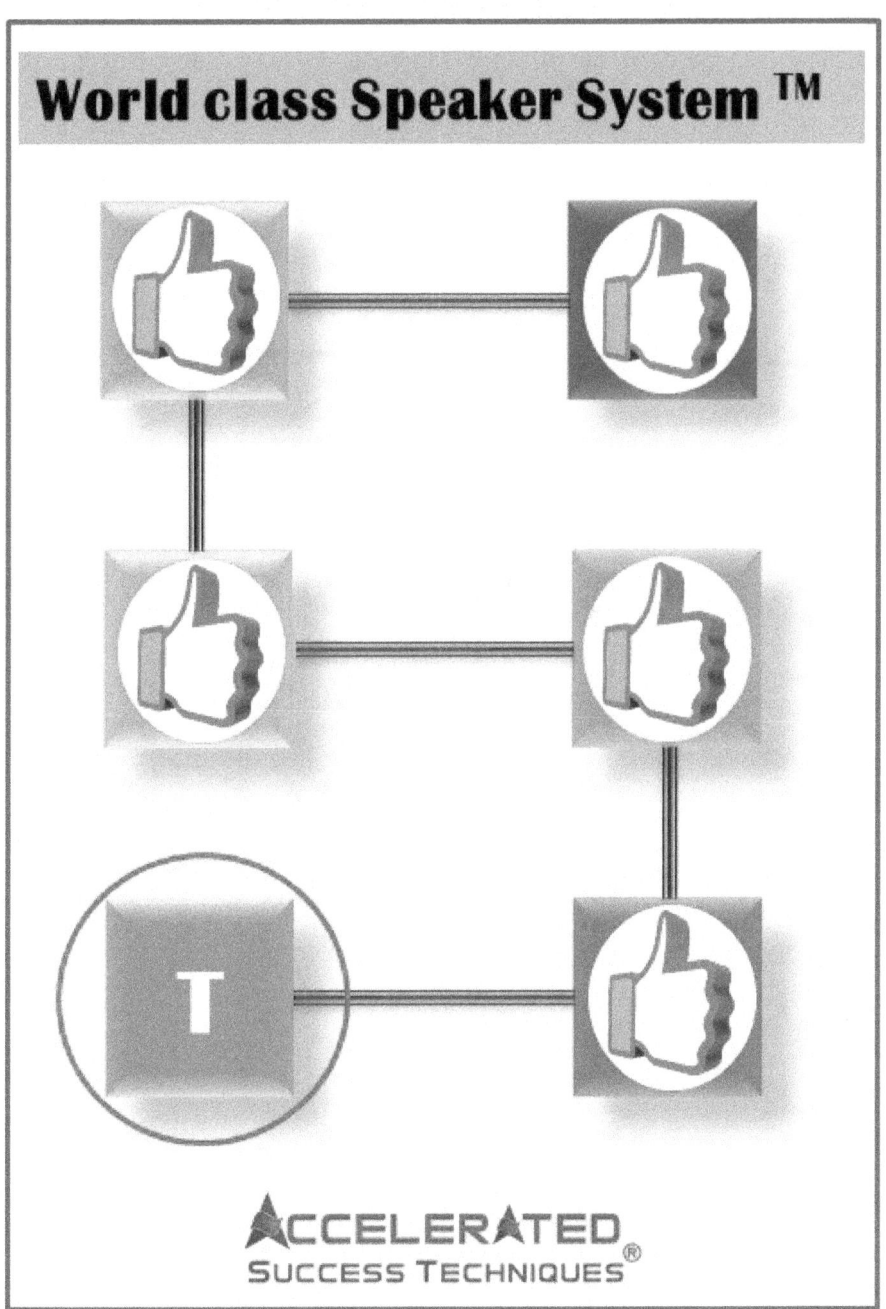

© Success Coach Nilesh

7 Steps in Public Speaking

1   Master Your **TOPIC**

The biggest mistake new speakers do is that they try to speak on a topic they feel like talking rather than a topic they are expert in.

I have done this mistake too.

I used to check newspapers, magazines and internet to choose any hot or trending topics. I failed to realize that I am not an expert in each and every topic.

I also learnt one more thing.
When I share 3 points about a topic to the audience, I must know 10 things about it. If you want to be seen as an expert in your field then you must **know more than you speak.**

This will also help you when any questions are raised by your audience. You are now well prepared and being an expert you have earned the right to speak on the chosen topic.

Now the question arises-How to select your topic?

Here are two ways you can try:
1) Speak on a topic you know more about, from your past experiences, education, knowledge etc.

2) Choose a topic you love to speak on. You should spend time to know more and more about the topic and once you have enough information to write a small book on the topic, you can then give a short speech on the topic. That's right, know more than you speak.

Never ever speak on the topic you are new to.

The 2nd Step = Identify your REASON to speak

Don't speak to Impress; Speak to Express. Impression will take care on its own.

~ Success Coach Nilesh

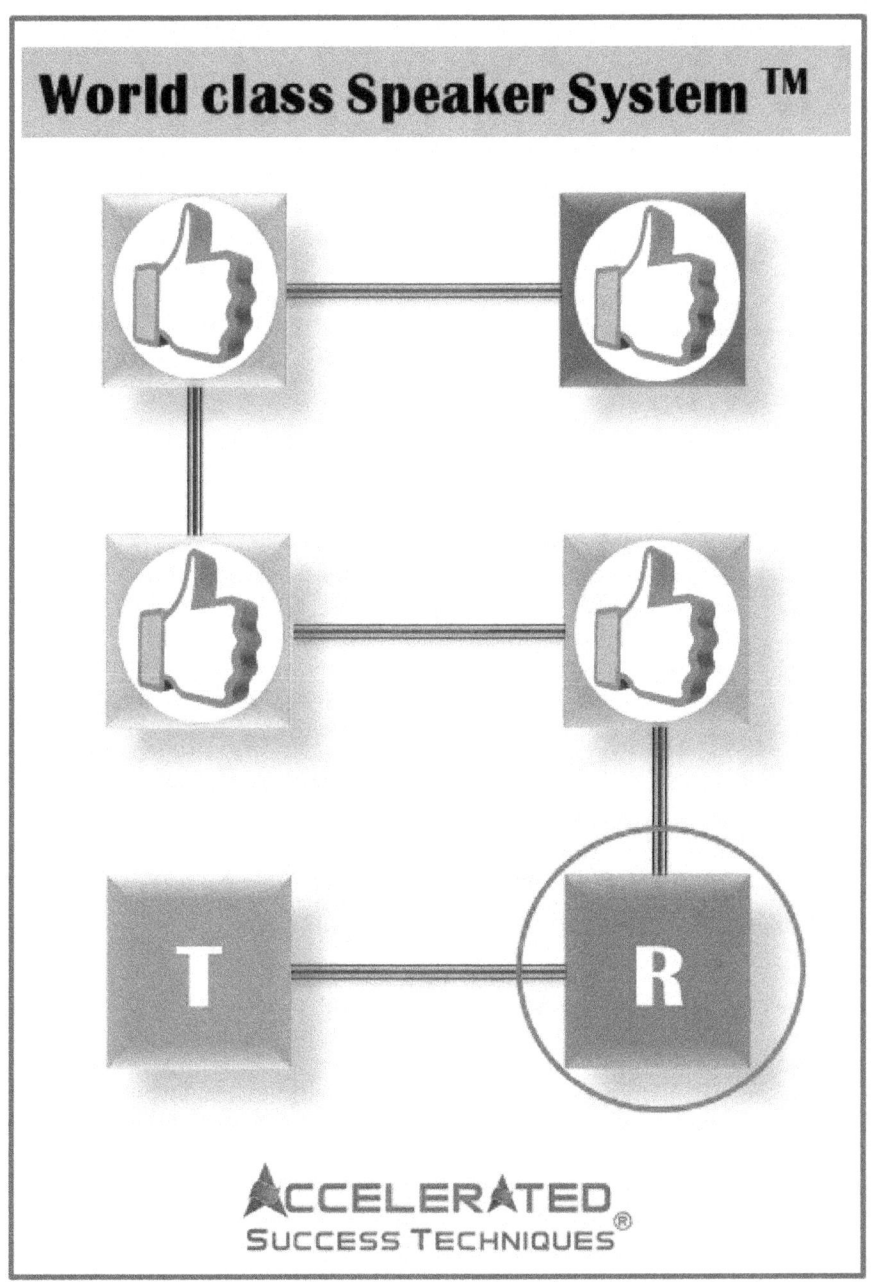

© Success Coach Nilesh

7 Steps in Public Speaking

1 Master Your **TOPIC**

Identify your **REASON** to speak **2**

There is a famous saying, "If your WHY is big then HOW is not a problem"

WHY is the reason and HOW is the process.

If you know your reason to speak then your mind will help you navigate to your ultimate goal of speaking.

Is your aim to motivate the audience?
Is your aim to inform something to audience?
Is your aim to move them emotionally?
Is your aim to get them take any action?
Is your aim to entertain the audience?
Is your aim to get them buy something from you?

Whatever might be your aim,
Be clear about it.

It will help you generate the ideas and share relevant examples & activities during your speech.

The 3rd Step = Design your speech SKELETON

Don't memorize your speech word by word. Memorize Bullet points and its sequence.

~ Success Coach Nilesh

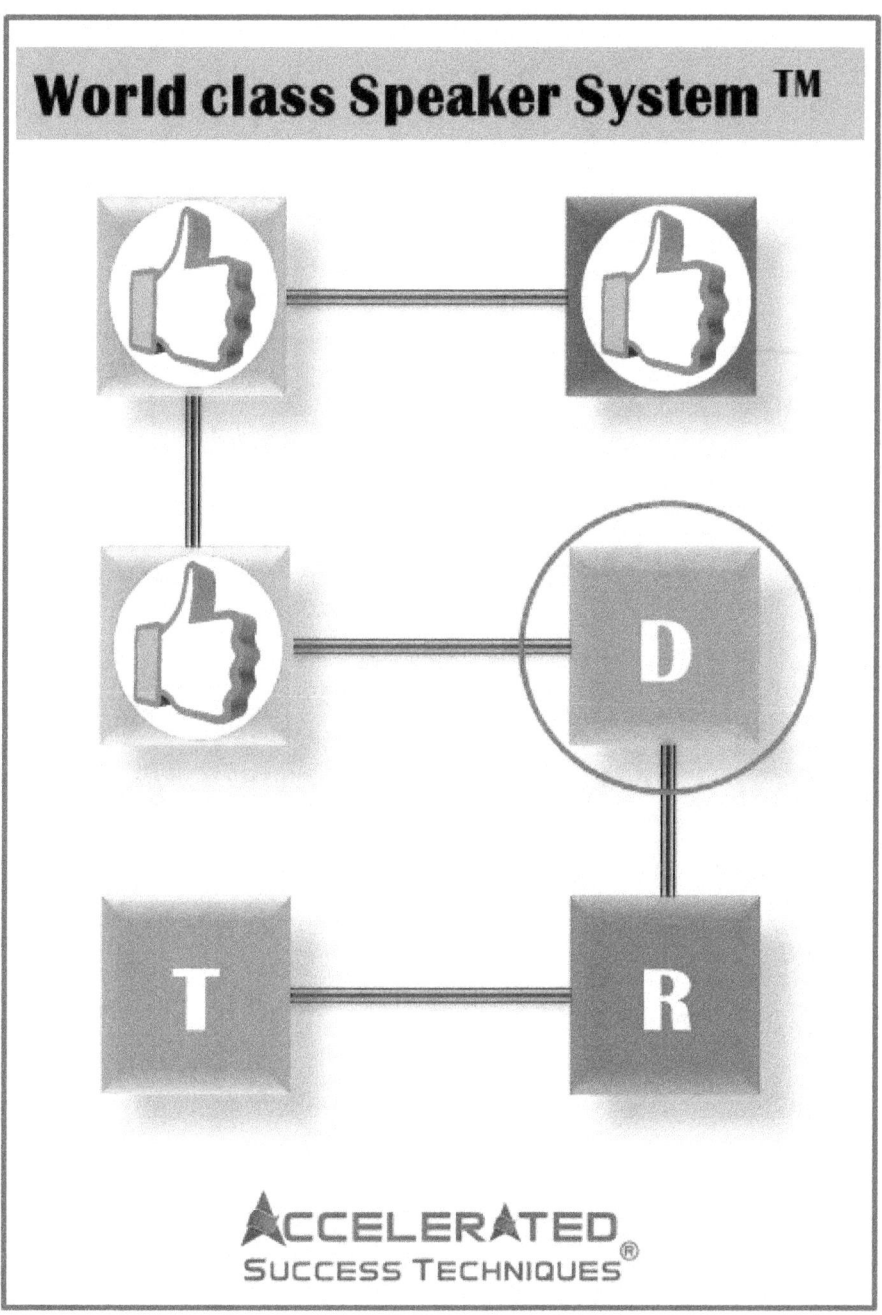

© Success Coach Nilesh

7 Steps in Public Speaking

1 Master Your **TOPIC**

Identify your **REASON** to speak **2**

3 Design your speech **SKELETON**

I used to think speech is a collection of words and sentences rather than a well-designed format. After listening to world class speakers I realized that I was wrong.

Powerful speech is a well-designed speech.
Influential speech is a well-designed speech.

So how to design your speech?

Well-designed speech has 3 parts.

(1) START
(2) BODY
(3) END (also called as Conclusion)

START:
There are variety of ways you can start your speech. E.g. Start with a story, start by asking questions, start with quotes etc.
The key for a powerful start is to hook the listeners' attention.

If you can capture their attention at the start, 40% of the job is done.
Listeners will stay with you.
They would want to know more about you or your topic.

BODY:
This is the main part of the speech.
Explain your ideas one by one here.

I would suggest that if you are new to speaking then write down 3-5 ideas you want to share with your audience. Each idea is your one bullet point. Now find out at least one example to support your bullet point. Your example can be a past experience, a short story you know or may be an activity. Choose whatever suits best to the context.

END:
After body, the most important part of a speech is 'end' or in other words conclusion.

Your audience will always remember this.

You can use a story or a quote or a pondering question. Whatever it is; design it to be memorable.

Remember this:

In your Speech:
START must Hook
Body must Engage and
END must be Memorable

This design will make your speech very effective and powerful.

The 4th Step = Visualize your Success

Don't worry about your speech; Take care of it.

~ Success Coach Nilesh

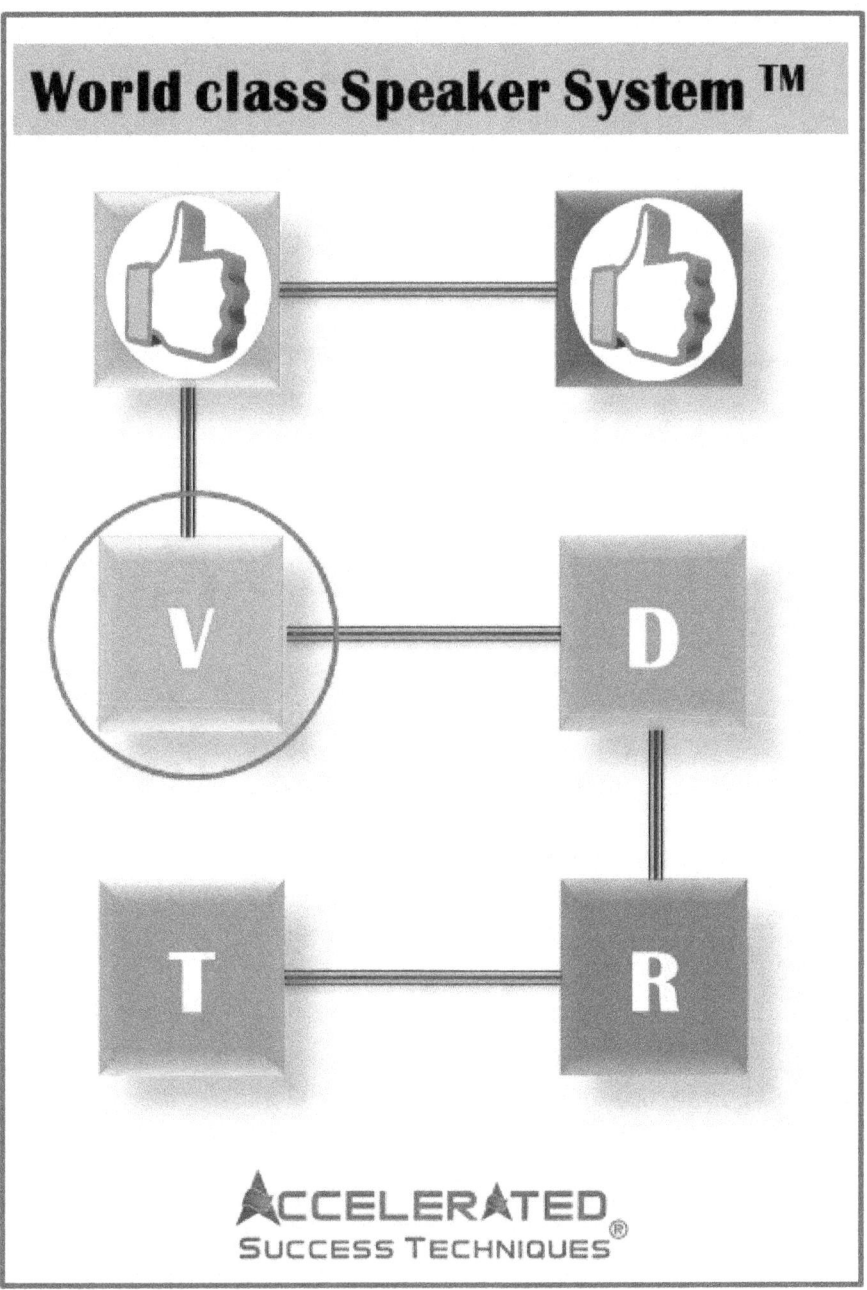

© Success Coach Nilesh

As human beings, we have received a wonderful gift and that is the gift of ability to Visualize.
Visualization is a tool where you imagine and let the creativity flow in your brain.

In professional speaking you can use this tool to regain confidence, calm down your anxiety and make your speech powerful.

Successful speakers use this tool.

Go ahead. Try it.

Once you have designed your speech, find a place where no one will disturb you and close your eyes. Take deep breaths (two to three times) and start your imagination.

Imagine that you have dressed perfectly for your speech and now you are stepping up on the stage to speak. The audience is clapping and giving you a warm welcome.

You start speaking and proceed with your flow of speech.
Say what you have to say. Watch your body postures while sharing your powerful message. See yourself ending the speech with memorable words. See that the audience has given you the best possible standing ovation and they are cheering with your name.

Just go ahead and try it.

You'll experience two things.

Either your mind will let you imagine all this or it will hold you at some points.

Make a note of all these holding points. This is exactly what we want.

Our mind knows, internally, what you are confident at and what can be your weaknesses. It will reveal those points in the visualization process.

Your job now is to go back to your speech preparation and improve your weaknesses.

Then redo the visualization.

Repeat the process UNTIL you feel the confidence.

Once you feel the confidence inside you, it is easy to confidently deliver the speech.

Visualization is a very effective tool.

The 5th Step = Stay Genuine

Don't try to be second rate of someone else when you can become first class of your own.
~ Success Coach Nilesh

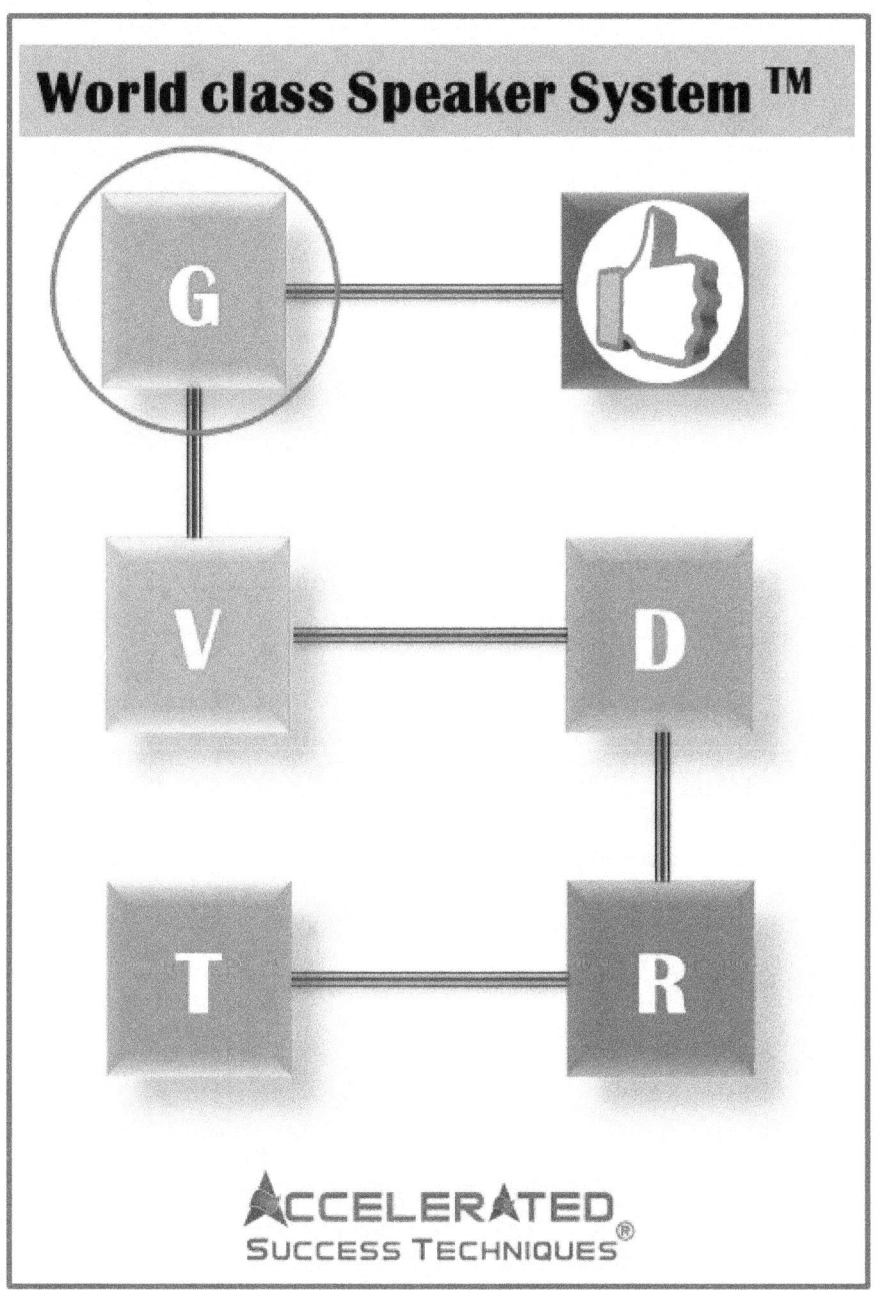

© Success Coach Nilesh

7 Steps in Public Speaking

1 Master Your **TOPIC**

Identify your **REASON** to speak 2

3 Design your speech **SKELETON**

VISUALIZE your success 4

5 Stay **GENUINE**

You are who you are.

You are Unique.

There is nobody like you.

You have your unique way.
You have your unique method.
You have your unique stance.
You have your unique tone.
You have your unique accent.
You have your unique body language.

Use it.

Sadly, many new speakers forget it.

Don't try to be like someone else who you are not.
Audience can easily recognize that.

Don't try to be second rate of someone else when you can become first class of your own.

Learn from others but be yourself.
The genuine fellow.

When you are genuine and not copying someone else, your audience will feel you. The real you.

They will easily connect with you. Therefore as a speaker it will make your job easy to play full out and share your transformational message.

The 6th Step = Connect & Deliver

Secret to powerful communication is that it begins with connection.

~ Success Coach Nilesh

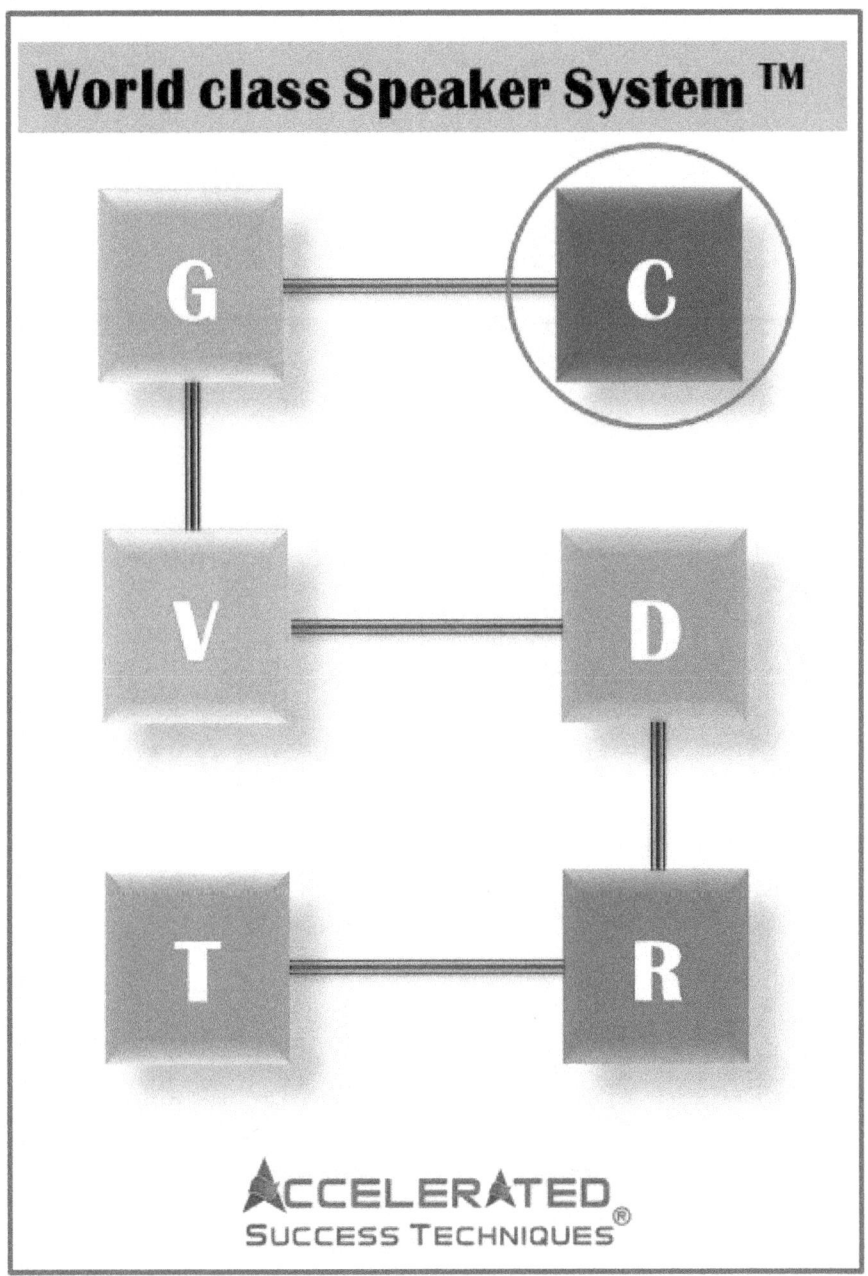

© Success Coach Nilesh

Have you ever spoken over telephone?

You may ask what a dumb question it was, but let me go further.

When you speak with someone over telephone; the very first thing that has to happen is that your call must get connected.

Until it gets connected, you can't share any information with the person on the other side.

This is exactly similar to 'speaking professionally'.

The only difference here is that, it is you on one side and your audience on the other.

Public speaking, communication or presentation is not a one way activity.

To be an influential speaker you must connect with the audience first and then share your message.

Otherwise, the audience will get bored, confused and will just wait for you to finish your speech.

So how to connect with your audience?

Here are the 3 simple techniques to get you started:
1) Identify WHY the audience has come for. What do they want and what are they looking for? Then make your speech content **relevant** to them. They will be able to connect with you.

Before I start my speech, I always study about my audience. It helps me design my speech which is most relevant to needs of the audience.

2) Choose your attire and body language suitable to your audience. Wear formals for formal events and casuals for informal events.

3) Smile and make use of humor. There is a famous quote saying, **"A smile is a curve that sets everything straight"**.

When your audience sees your smiling and fresh face they automatically get a better feeling about the person and if you use humor during the speech you will win the audience. They will love you.

Now,
coming to the delivery of the speech.

So far if you have followed steps 1-6, you will have wonderful content plus a powerful way to start your speech. Now your job is to stand up, go on the stage you were waiting for and deliver the content in the sequence: Start-Body-End.

That's it.

There is no magical success formula than to **Just do it**.

It doesn't matter how much you prepare, a little anxiety about your speech will still remain. It's natural.

Let it happen.

Worry will hold you back. **Preparation** and **Focus** will take you ahead.

Don't worry.

Focus on Audience and the value you are going to add to the life, career or business of each person present in your audience.

The 7th Step = Keep Moving Forward

Become better, every day.

~   Success Coach Nilesh

© Success Coach Nilesh

Do you want a lot of Success as a Professional Speaker?

Do you want to reach a lot of audience and help them transform their lives for the better?

If yes,

Then this 7th step will help you achieve your dreams.

As you know the famous saying, **"Rome wasn't built in a day"**

It takes time to become world-class.

It takes time to master your craft.

It takes time to get paid a high amount as a speaker.

However,

If you want to accelerate your journey to success then this 7th step will help you.

It's called as **"Keep Moving Forward"**.

On your journey to success you will experience many odd things such as not enough people are coming to your seminars or workshop, you are not able to charge the ticket prices you want, you are not getting booked as a speaker, you are not able to develop new and powerful content, you are not able to market your services effectively, people around you starts to doubt on your capabilities, you are not doing very well financially, you are struggling to make your content more engaging and fun, You are afraid of failing on the stage etc.

 However the only thing which can help you proceed is the tag line and the attitude of **"Keep Moving Forward"** in spite of all problems.

When I first started my speaking business, I was anxious and naive at how hard it would be to get my first client. I knew for sure that there would be a lot of hard work, phone calls, and meetings. But that seemed to go nowhere. No one told me that it would end up taking me 5 months until I finally got my first client. If I had seen all the challenges and obstacles to getting that first client up front, I might have lost my nerve and looked for easier path. However I would have ultimately missed, what I really had dreamed of all along.

I had set a worthy goal for myself of starting a consulting business from the ground up. I had a dream that I was passionate about. I had honed my skills and qualifications enough that I knew I had a solid chance. I had a SMART Action List and worked my game plan day in and day out. However, for all of this, I did not yet know how to land a customer. I had met with plenty of professionals in my field, connected with other passionate people, and even spent time learning from people who had gone before. However, none of this could guarantee success in the one thing that I most needed that is getting a paying customer on the books!

Five months of knocking on doors and calling an endless web of referrals and connections seemed to be in vain. However, I had determined from the start to **do one thing and do it well**, and to learn from my mistakes and failures.

Every time I got a "No" from someone, I would sit down and re-evaluate what I did. I would analyze my overall approach. This was sometimes a painful process. Often, at the beginning, my emotional mind would start to take over and I would think, "What on earth am I doing? I can't do this. This is bound to fail. I'll never get a client. I'll never get the money I need …" However, I would push my emotional and logical sides to work together and come up with a better plan to fight back. Every single time, I would come up with some new approach to solve the problem that I had never tried before. And for 5 months, every single time, it would fail to result in a client.

I still remember an email message from my friend Praveen. He had mentioned, "Nilesh, Don't be a workaholic. Be a resultoholic" and something snapped in my mind.

That one day, I sat down with a potential client like I had a million times before, but this time I changed my approach to conduct my business meetings. I started with questions instead of information about my products, and then I precisely gave him specific solutions. That day, I left the table with success. And I've been successful many, many times since.

What had happened over the course of those many months was a continual process of improvement that has not stopped to this day. After every failure, I would go back and look for improvement. I would let the pain of that failure fuel my determination to do whatever it took to hone my skills and attributes. Sometimes, I would walk through the entire process over again and double-check not only my methods, but also my very dreams and desires. Time and time again, I had adapted and changed things in little and planned ways, until one day, I met with success.

There's no failure that you can't learn from. I believe that we only truly fail when we allow our present lack of success to cause us to give up on our dreams. Many people see success stories and successful people and think that they've obtained some level that makes them immune to failure. As I learned, however, this could not be further from the truth. To this day, I continue to fail, but as many times as I fail, I continue to improve as well. What I've learnt through this continual process of improvement is exactly what I've already shared in this book.

My success rate now is quite high for this very reason. **I keep going until I find a way to make it happen.**

In this final chapter, I want to impart three important lessons which has made massive contributions to my success.

First lesson: Get back on track at the very next opportunity.

Being raised from failure to success, in many occasions I found myself losing the success track. There were many reasons. Sometimes I was not focused, sometimes the task was too hard that it knocked me off the track, sometimes it took longer than the expected time to complete some tasks, or sometimes some unknown emergency hit me. But then I deliberately chose to stay on my success track. The next day, I used to read my goals and decide on the things to do to move towards my ultimate success. Then I just took those steps. Now I've been knocked out many times; however, <u>I've made a comeback every single time.</u>

Therefore, if you find yourself losing the success track, **just don't blame yourself.** Forgive yourself and get back on track at the very next opportunity.

Second lesson: Power of momentum.

Momentum works like magic. At the beginning, it may seem overwhelming to do so many things, but as you get into flow, you catch up the momentum and then you'll find yourself doing so many things, with fun and in a shorter period.

Can you remember the feeling when you were learning to drive a car? At the beginning, there were too many things to look after. You needed to pay attention to mirrors, gears, pedestrians, rules, breaks, steering, etc. But as you kept going, many things became subconscious and then you didn't even realize that you're doing so many mirror checks or clutch-gear shifting in fraction of a second. It seems like you didn't even worry about it.

Therefore, it's very important to reach to this phase of momentum. So <u>start early, never mind about making mistakes and then get into the momentum.</u> It will accelerate your journey. It's an essential part of your learning curve.

Third lesson: Continual improvement process.

My continual improvement process is made-up of two rules:

Rule # 1: Get better than yesterday, even if it's as small as 0.01%.

Rule # 2: Follow Rule 1 every day.

This may seem like a very small improvement, but if you pile that up, it has a compound effect. Every day you become a better and a more skillful person.

It's a simple tool to refocus your efforts and learn from your failures. Whether you're still hunting for that first client or sitting at the pinnacle of success, I believe that this tool will help you to improve and find greater levels of success.

Before Saying Goodbye

Public Speaking is a skill.
Just like any other skill you can master it.

It's similar to learning to drive or cook.
At first it seems difficult however once you know the key points; you get the confidence.

To master this skill, you will have to re do the process several times.

My friend,
now you know the 7 key steps to start speaking professionally.

Use these steps.

Share it with your friends who also want to improve their communication, presentation and public speaking skills. Connect with growth oriented people like you.

If you get at least one passionate learning buddy, you will experience that you are progressing faster towards your goal.

All the Best.

Yours Truly,

Success Coach Nilesh

© Success Coach Nilesh

© Success Coach Nilesh

Additional Success Resources for YOU

What you read SHAPES what you think and what you think SHAPES what you achieve in your life.

Thank you for choosing this book. This will transform your life.

~   Success Coach Nilesh

<u>Other</u> Best Selling Success Resources <u>for you</u>

<u>Proudly Marketed and Sold by</u>

Major online book retailers & www.SuccessCoachNilesh.com

Grab your copy

Read them – Gift them – Recommend them

www.ingramcontent.com/pod-product-compliance
Lightning Source LLC
Chambersburg PA
CBHW070821180526
45168CB00002B/709